P9-CQL-453

About the Book

An ostrich stands a foot tall a few days after birth and grows to about eight feet at maturity, making it one of the tallest birds in the world and, with its long legs, one of the swiftest of animals.

Still unhatched, Ozzie learns to identify his parents' booming voices. After birth and throughout his young life, he will stay close to them, learning what to eat, how to detect danger, and where to find water and developing his keen sight.

Ozzie's first survival of the dry season on the great African veld and his magnificent, astonishing courtship of his first mate make a fascinating narrative, full of beautiful descriptions and interesting facts about this unusual bird.

Biography of an

OSTRICH

by ALICE L. HOPF
ILLUSTRATED BY BEN F. STAHL

G. P. Putnam's Sons   New York

CULVER MILITARY ACADEMY LIBRARY

Text copyright © 1974 by Alice Hopf
Illustrations copyright © 1974 by Ben Stahl
All rights reserved. Published simultaneously in
Canada by Longman Canada Limited, Toronto.
SBN: GB-399-60839-7
SBN: TR-399-20350-8
Library of Congress Catalog Card Number: 72-95562
PRINTED IN THE UNITED STATES OF AMERICA
07210

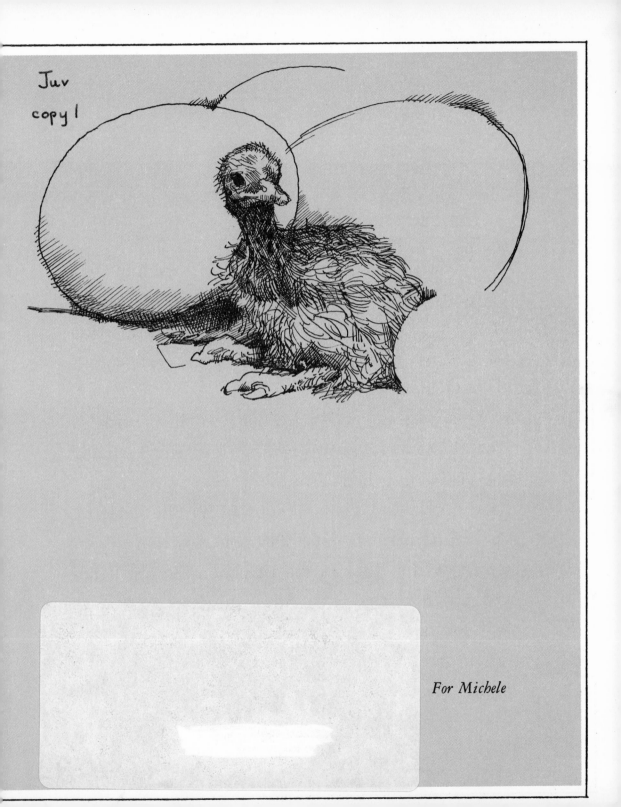

Juv
copy 1

For Michele

On the dry African veld, a father ostrich made his nest. He had dug a round hole in the sand of a dry riverbed. Every year he brought the hens of his family to his nest. Every year they all laid their eggs in it.

This year he had three hens in his family. The oldest one was top hen ostrich. She pushed the two young hens around. If they tried to sit on the nest, she chased them away. She herself sat on the nest all day. The father ostrich kept watch nearby. Late in the afternoon the top hen got up from the nest. She wandered away to look for food on the veld. Then the father ostrich sat on the nest. He sat there all through the night. He was a good and careful father ostrich.

There were twenty-two eggs in the nest. Most of them had been laid by the top hen ostrich. The two younger hens each laid only four or five eggs. Ostriches are the largest birds in the world. And they lay the largest eggs. An ostrich egg may weigh as much as three pounds!

The African veld is a kind of desert with grass and low thorny bushes. In some places there are trees. But when there is no rain, everything dries up. All the animals gather near the few water holes. There are many trails leading to the water holes. Near one of these trails the father ostrich had made his nest. When he wanted a drink, he ran along the trail to the water hole. Then he followed the trail back to the nest. He did not get lost in the great wide veld.

Other animals followed the trail to the water hole: antelopes and zebras, lions and jackals. But they did not see the ostrich nest nearby. If the ostriches left their nest, they covered the eggs with sand. When an ostrich sat on the nest, she stretched her long neck out on the ground. Her head lay in the desert grass. Her round body looked just like a desert rock. Nobody knew that an ostrich was sitting on its eggs.

It takes a long time for an ostrich egg to hatch. The parent birds sat on their eggs for forty to forty-five days. But before the first egg hatched, they knew that their babies were alive. The little chicks inside the eggs began to peep. The mother and father ostriches put their heads down close to the eggs and peeped back. Even before the baby birds hatched, they learned to know their parents' voices.

Little Ozzie was curled up inside the egg. He had grown so much that there was no room left in the shell. His beak was pushed right up against his foot, and he was beginning to feel very uncomfortable. He heard the peeping of his mother outside and of the other chicks inside the other eggs. So he gave a big push with the strong muscles of his neck. There was a sharp popping noise, and a hole like a window broke in the shell of the egg. Ozzie lay in the egg and looked out of the hole. He rested for a while and then began to peck at the sides of the window. After another rest, he made a great effort. He pushed with both his neck and his legs. All at once the shell flew apart. It broke into many pieces. Ozzie was free. He stretched out his neck and gave a very loud peep—a call of triumph. He was the first chick to hatch out of its egg.

Ozzie was content to lie in the nest all that day. More and more chicks began to hatch out of their eggs. They rested under their mother while their downy feathers dried, peeping to each other. Every once in a while the mother peeped back. In the evening, Father Ostrich came to sit on the nest. He peeped to his new chicks and called to them in a deep, harsh voice. They began to learn his different calls.

In a day or two all the chicks had hatched. The nest was so full that some were pushed outside. Ozzie was the first to climb out. He poked his head from under his mother's feathers and climbed out onto the sand. When he stood up and stretched his neck, he was almost a foot tall.

Soon after Ozzie began to take his first uncertain steps, he was running about on the sand close to the nest. If he got too far away, his mother called and he ran back again. Nearby in the grass sat his father. He was watching for danger. He watched the nearby trail for animals going to the water hole and up in the air for dangerous birds. He stretched his neck and peered across the veld. At the least sign of danger, he called a deep *boo,* and all the chicks ran back under their mother's wings.

As soon as Ozzie could walk, he began to peck at everything he saw on the sandy ground. He had to learn what was good to eat. He even picked up tiny stones and swallowed them. But the stones were good for him, too. They went into his stomach and helped digest the food that he was eating.

When all the eggs had hatched, the mother got up from the nest. Calling and cheeping, she led the little ones away across the veld. The father ostrich went with them, calling all the time to keep the large family together. The two younger hens followed along. All the big ostriches moved carefully and stretched their long necks to watch for danger. But the father ostrich had the longest neck and the best eyes. He could see far, far across the veld. Little Ozzie followed his father and mother. Their images were imprinted on his tiny brain. He would always know them from all other ostriches and animals.

Father Ostrich was nearly eight feet tall. His long neck and legs were bare, and the feathers on his body were black. The beautiful plumes on his wings and tail were white and curly. He did not use them for flying, but for dancing and showing off. Ostriches are so big and heavy that they cannot fly. But they can run more than forty miles per hour, faster than most animals. They have very long, strong legs with only two toes. The hen ostriches are brown with lighter shades on their plumes. And all the adult ostriches have thick black eyelashes.

The ostrich family wandered across the veld. Now that all the chicks had hatched, they would not return to the nest for another year. They moved back and forth across the desert. They went wherever they could find food and water. Ostriches will eat almost anything. They like insects and lizards or seeds and fruit and flowers.

Little Ozzie picked at everything he saw. Soon he was picking up seeds and bugs, as well as little pebbles. He ran about through the tough grass of the veld. When he got too far away, his father called *boo!* Quickly he ran back to his family. But if his father called *boo! boo!* in a different tone, Ozzie knew it meant danger. He stopped what he was doing and stood perfectly still. Sometimes he lay down with his head and neck flat on the ground. His round body and baby feathers looked just like a clump of desert grass.

46037

One day Father Ostrich called *boo! boo!* and all the baby chicks froze where they were. Even the hen ostriches squatted down and tried to look like rocks. The danger was very near. Father Ostrich began to run and cry out. He was dragging his wings in the dust. He seemed to be in great pain and trouble. Just then a huge, tawny animal walked right past Ozzie. The little ostrich did not know it was a lioness. But he knew enough to be afraid. He kept very still.

The lioness knew that Father Ostrich was only pretending to be hurt to distract her. She paid no attention. She walked on, looking for anything that moved. Suddenly she fell over one of the chicks. The baby ostrich tried to run, but the lioness pounced. The chick gave one loud peep and was still. The lioness ran off with it in her jaws. Not until the hen ostriches peeped several times, did Little Ozzie get up and run back to the family.

The top hen ostrich led the way through the desert. She knew the best places for taking dust baths. She knew where the wild figs were ripe. She told the family when it was safe to go forward and when they should run away. Sometimes one of the younger hens tried to go first. Then the top hen chased her back. She pecked her and flapped her wings at her. The younger hen went back and walked behind.

The top hen knew when it was the right time to go to the water hole. Many animals use the few water holes in the desert. The shiest of them all are the ostriches. They wait until the other animals have finished drinking. They are very careful not to go when dangerous animals may be there.

Sometimes the ostrich family moved about with flocks of friendly animals. Antelopes, zebras, and giraffes are all vegetarians. They are friendly to the ostriches. All these animals move along together, looking for food on the veld.

The ostrich and the giraffe have very long necks. They can see much farther than the other animals. They can see enemies when they are still far off across the veld. The other animals watch them as they are eating. If the ostrich starts to run, all the other animals run, too. Their enemies cannot sneak up on them and catch them.

The ostriches often join the flocks of antelopes and zebras because these animals help them find food. As they move across the veld, eating what grass they can find, they scare up the insects. And the ostriches are right behind them. They see the grasshoppers fly up. Their quick beaks stab, and they swallow the juicy tidbit. Ozzie soon learned this was a good way to find food.

One day when he heard the danger signal, Ozzie stood still and looked over the grass tops. Off to one side he saw the top hen and Father Ostrich putting on their "crippled bird" act. They ran back and forth, calling in distress. Their wings dragged on the ground and sometimes fluttered helplessly. When the enemy did not follow, Father Ostrich dropped to the ground and whirled about. He beat his wings and made a great noise.

Then Ozzie saw the enemy. It was a jackal, and it was paying no attention to Father Ostrich. It too knew about the ostrich distraction display. It was running about with its nose to the ground, trying to find the chicks. Ozzie pulled his neck down as low as he could. He did not dare lie down now. Any movement would be seen by the jackal. Ozzie remembered the chick that the lion had caught. He was terribly afraid.

Then Father Ostrich stopped pretending he was hurt. He ran up to the jackal. He put down his long neck and hissed. The jackal stopped in surprise. It wasn't sure what to do. It snarled and got ready to jump. But Father Ostrich's big leg shot out. His foot caught the jackal and hurled it back across the veld. The jackal landed in a thorn bush. All the big ostriches stretched out their necks and hissed. The jackal ran off with its tail between its legs. Then the top hen called the chicks and led them quickly away.

Little Ozzie was a foot tall when he came out
of the egg, and he grew almost a foot each
month. By the time he was five months old he
was five feet tall and could run almost as fast as
his parents. But he still stayed close to his family. He still went where the top hen led them,
and he kept very quiet when he heard his father
call *boo!*

When the dry season came, there was less
and less to eat in the ostrich family's territory.
The top hen led the group to a large water hole
that almost never dried up. Many animals came
here to find food and water. There were herds
of gnus and gazelles. There were zebras and
giraffes and many kinds of antelope. There were
also predators that killed and ate these animals
—lions and leopards and jackals.

There were many ostrich families staying near the big water hole. They made a large flock. They lived together during the dry season. Ozzie came to know these strangers and felt safe among them. He was no longer a little chick and could run as fast as any adult ostrich. He knew what was good to eat. He could take care of himself. In the large flock of several hundred ostriches, Ozzie began to move about with other young birds of his own age.

It takes an ostrich three years to become mature and ready to have his own family. Ozzie had been to the water hole three times in three dry seasons before he took special note of a young female ostrich from another family. By now he was almost as tall as his father and had grown beautiful white plumes on his wings and tail. They showed in great contrast with the black feathers on his body. Ozzie was a handsome bird, and when he stood next to the smaller, brown female while they grazed, she did not move away.

For once, Ozzie forgot to pay attention to what was going on around him. All the ostriches were moving in a slow circle around the water hole, picking up insects that the antelopes kicked up. Suddenly there was a disturbance near them. A pied crow sprang into the air, cawing its alarm cry. All the animals and birds stood at attention. Somewhere there was danger. Somewhere very near.

All at once the herds began to run. The young female ostrich was frightened and confused. She began to run away from the flock. She would get lost. Ozzie ran faster than the hen and ran in front of her. He began to wave his great white wings. The hen saw his signal. She turned and ran after him. He led her in a big circle back to the flock and away from danger.

After that Brownie was his special hen. The two birds fed together and slept near each other. Whenever there was danger, Brownie followed the signal of Ozzie's white, curly wings.

Now other young male ostriches began to look at Brownie. One big cock from Brownie's own family, who already had two hens following him around, came every day and flirted with Brownie. He walked up and down in front of her and showed off his new adult feathers. He stood up very tall with his tail pointing up. The skin on his face and legs turned red, and he hissed and snorted at any nearby bird. Then he tried to chase Brownie around, holding his wings very high and waving first one and then the other at her.

Ozzie did not like this at all. Brownie was his hen. His face also blushed bright red and he snorted back. *Boo! Boo!* he rumbled, sounding very much like his father when he chased the jackal. Ozzie danced right up to the big male ostrich, waving his wings and snorting. His long neck shot back and forth like a snake. He was looking for a good place to strike the other with his sharp beak.

The other male decided Brownie was not worth a fight. He already had two young hens of his own. He began to back away. Ozzie followed him. Soon Ozzie was chasing the other ostrich, snorting and hissing as he went. When they had gone far enough, Ozzie went back to Brownie. Little by little, he led her away to another part of the flock.

A few days later Ozzie wandered away from the flock and the water hole. The dry season was breaking. Soon there would be rain and the families would separate again. But this year Ozzie would not go with his old family. He remembered a nice sandy spot in a hollow with a large thorn bush guarding it. He had noticed it when he passed it several months ago. But now it had a special meaning for him. He hoped he could find the hollow again. Yes, there was the thorn bush to show him the way!

Ozzie ran down into the little hollow and began to dig with his feet in the sand. It was almost as though he were dusting. But Ozzie dug much deeper than he would for a dust bath. He dug out a big round hole. He got out of it and looked at it, and then he dug some more. When at last he was satisfied with it, he went to find Brownie.

CULVER MILITARY ACADEMY
LIBRARY

Flashing his white wings, Ozzie led Brownie away from the flock. He led her to his hole. Brownie looked at the hole. Ozzie walked all around it. Brownie followed him. They both looked at the hole. Then Ozzie began his court-ship display.

He put his head down and said *Boo . . . boo . . . boooooh-hoo!* It was a booming sound. It could be heard far across the veld. It told other ostriches to stay away from this nesting place. It told his hen ostrich that this would be the place where she would lay her eggs. Ozzie began to walk around and around the nest, flashing his wings in a right-left display. Suddenly, he dropped to the ground and whirled around and around in a nesting display, with his beautiful feathers sweeping the sand. His long neck twisted around also in a corkscrew motion. *Boo . . . boo . . .* he called.

Brownie watched Ozzie's display. Now and then she stopped to pull some grass from the veld. But she always came back to look at what he was doing. At last she, too, put down her head and crouched on the ground. The two ostriches were ready to mate.

Now the flocks were breaking up around the water hole. Every day there were fewer ostriches there. Ozzie and Brownie stayed by their nest. They went to the water hole only to drink. Every day Brownie laid an egg in the nest Ozzie had made. She was a young hen, and she laid only six eggs, but Ozzie started to sit on them at once. He sat all night and part of the afternoon. In the morning Brownie sat so that Ozzie could graze nearby. He never went far and he kept a careful watch for danger.

At last one afternoon, Ozzie heard the first peep-peep from inside the eggs. He put his head down close to the egg and peeped back. These were his first eggs and his first chicks and he was going to care for them and defend them with all the strength and skill of a male ostrich.

Ozzie would probably live to be fifty years old. In the future he would dance longer and fight harder. He would have more hens in his family and many more eggs in his nest. He would do his best to survive in the African wild.

The Author

Alice L. Hopf is equally at home writing science fiction (under her maiden name, A. M. Lightner) and writing about nature. She has written several nature and animal books for Putnam, including *Biography of an Octopus, Biography of a Rhino*, and *Biography of an Ant*. Mrs. Hopf resides in New York City.

The Artist

Coming from a family of artists, *Ben F. Stahl* is a painter, teacher, and illustrator. He was born in Chicago, studied at the California School of Fine Arts, and from 1964 to 1967 was the director of art education at the Famous Artists School in Amsterdam, Holland. He lives with his wife, Carolyn, and their four children in Weston, Connecticut.